Offer Him All Things,
Charred, Burned & Cindered

Kala is the author of the poetry collection, *He Is Honey, Salt and the Most Perfect Grammar* (2016) and two novels, *Mahasena* and *Theivanai* (parts one and two of the Murugan Trilogy; 2021 and 2024). She lives in Bangalore with Paru, Gauri, Sathyavak and Totoro.

Offer Him All Things, Charred, Burned & Cindered

KALA KRISHNAN

cntxt

First published by Context, an imprint of Westland Publications Private Limited, in 2018

Published by Context, an imprint of Westland Books, a division of Nasadiya Technologies Private Limited, in 2024

No. 269/2B, First Floor, 'Irai Arul', Vimalraj Street, Nethaji Nagar, Alapakkam Main Road, Maduravoyal, Chennai 600095

Westland, the Westland logo, Context and the Context logo are the trademarks of Nasadiya Technologies Private Limited, or its affiliates.

ISBN: [◻]

10 9 8 7 6 5 4 3 2 1

Typeset in Meridien LT Std by Jojy Philip
Printed at [◻]

for

He Who Dwells in My HeartCave,
the one He invited in
&
Paru, Gauri, Sathyavak,
always

Contents

Introduction

You'd think it would be the same. After all, it is the same god and it should follow that he'd love the same things, but no: at Kataragama, he seems not as he is elsewhere. If Pazhani hill bent, as if he'd said *let the poets hold on, climb up*, in severe Kataragama, it seems as if he wants to shake them off.

His face says it all: the world is rising bile, he'd like to spit and be out of there before you can say his name. He wants none of this devotion or poetry; in fact, it's clear he wants nothing at all. Yet he waits, as if he's given word, so when you go to Kataragama, go lightly, for even before you start, he's tired of you already.

It's tough to say why he stokes poets' longing to come to Kataragama – it's evident he thinks that not one of us is going to measure up. In other places, our verse seems clever enough to bait this god, but at Kataragama, it is clear there is to be no time or space for the work of words, and no work at all, for poets.

His brother, the Elder, who rules over obstacles and turns and keeps things in/out – he's a much kinder god, and so poets' verses approach him for a beginning, a wave of the flags to Go! Perhaps the Elder will explain the younger's ways, for he knows his sibling as no one else does, in all his versions, the un-edited, too.

I don't know why the god of Kataragama – whose feet are set to run, waits for poets to come, like blank sheets. I don't know why I look to him, who turns away from things said, written & dreamt. Perhaps he wants to show how a poet can write praise of a god who sits on the ash-pile of this world. He knows what he's doing, for sure, and I know nothing. At Kataragama, if words turn to ash, ash may yet speak to me.

HE SITS ON THE ASH-PILE OF THE WORLD

Sutra

Sutra of offerings

Sutra 1

If you offer vetiver & sandal, he'll say, *I am partial to the smell of Tamizh.*

Sutra 2

If you offer holy chants, he'll say, *I am tired of hearing my own name.*

Sutra 3

If you offer fine cloths, he'll say, *I am no slip of the tongue, to be covered up.*

Sutra 4

If you offer crafted gold and silver, he'll say, *I am unalloyed treasure.*

Sutra 5

If you offer turmeric and salt, he'll say, *I am unfailing remedy and cure.*

Sutra 6

If you offer a lavish feast, he'll say, *I am in the mood to mendicate.*

Sutra 7

If you offer severe austerities, he'll say, *I'm inclined to sport and carouse.*

Sutra 8

If you offer festive drumming and dancing, he'll say, *I am not a roadshow.*

Sutra 9

If you offer the Vedas, he'll say, *I am in favour of the one over the many.*

Sutra 10

If you offer love, he'll say, *I am another name for love, haven't you heard?*

Sutra 11

If you ask him what he wants, he'll say, *I am sure the poets know – ask them.*

Sutra 12

If you want advice, take this: offer him all things charred, burned & cindered,
for this is Kataragama's Skanda, who likes to wear the worlds as flecks of ash.

Sutra of naming & doing

Sutra 1

Let it go: this naming keeps you – you and he – he.

Sutra 2

Let it stay: this naming makes you *mine* in his mouth.

Sutra 3

Hold it open: window and door it, this naming walks him in to.

Sutra 4

Slam it shut: latch & bolt it, this naming rooms him into.

Sutra 5

Ride it: touch it, leap astride it, bridle it, this naming is speedy mount.

Sutra 6

Cupboard it: roll it with neem & champa, this naming is timeless finery.

Sutra 7

Dry it: slice & spread it to sun, this naming is store against dearth.

Sutra 8

Will it: signature & witness it, this naming is timely inheritance.

Sutra 9

Accept it: beg it, bowl it, handful it, this naming is alms for all asks.

Sutra 10

Marry it: sleep with it, draw its seed, this naming is robust mating.

Sutra 11

Cultivate it: bury it, water it, this naming is germinating alphabets.

Sutra 12

Speak it: say Skanda, Lord of All, for this naming is deathless language.

Sutra of beseechment

Sutra 1

He charts earthly voyages: beseech him not to set your co-ordinates to Love.

Sutra 2

He tides the raging waters: beseech him not to weight your sails too light.

Sutra 3

He motors rain and wind: beseech him not to forget it is you they will buffet.

Sutra 4

He schedules storms and squalls: beseech him to give you a weatherly vessel.

Sutra 5

He sanctions marine battles: beseech him to be your auxiliary, guarantee refill.

Sutra 6

He worms rope lines: beseech him to let your vessel hold against Love's fleets.

Sutra 7

He wraps marline over: beseech him to be your asylum harbour, your distress dock.

Sutra 8

He canvas-covers rope: beseech him to teach you to wheel & deal, when the fight fails.

Sutra 9

He tompions the gun barrels: beseech him to avert your being taken prisoner of war.

Sutra 10

He mine-sweeps the waters: beseech him to dispatch expert teams to arbiter your release.

Sutra 11

He salvors the sunken: beseech him to reset co-ordinates, set you asail on a new page.

Sutra 12

He is Skanda, Lord of Kataragama: the far-sighted admiral who rosters poets' missions.

Sutra of Q & A

Sutra 1

Know this: If you ask him who he is, he will say, *I am the boss.*

Sutra 2

Know this: If you ask why you should be in his employ, he'll say, *why ever not?*

Sutra 3

Know this: If you ask for the terms of employment, he'll say, *whatever the contract says.*

Sutra 4

Know this: If you ask where the contract is, he'll say, *it's your job, you should know.*

Sutra 5

Know this: If you ask about employee benefits, he'll say, *if you're free, write them in.*

Sutra 6

Know this: If you ask about perks, he'll say, *we're all about profit; make them, split them.*

Sutra 7

Know this: If you ask him your official position, he'll say, *you'll head Drafts & Revisions.*

Sutra 8

Know this: If you ask him about severance and pension, he'll say, *we don't terminate.*

Sutra 9

Know this: If you ask him where the office is, he'll strike your chest and say, *right here.*

Sutra 10

Know this: If you ask for a calling-card, he'll give you one that reads *Poet, M/S Skanda & Co.*

Sutra 11

Know this: If you ask why he wants you, he'll say, *we're impressed with your text results.*

Sutra 12

Know this: Kataragama's Skanda wants his poets, singers & oracles to make their own contract.

Sutra of directions

Sutra 1

If you say he is the east, where the fire of the world ignites, he will stop, sputter and become west.

Sutra 2

If you say he is the west, where the fire goes to douse itself, he will spark, flame and turn into east.

Sutra 3

If you say he is the south, where death lurks, he will be north, where live the parents of the world.

Sutra 4

If you say he is the mountains at land's head, rising high, he will crouch, navel-low, and be Pazhani.

Sutra 5

If you say, he is straight ahead, no left–right, he will be a crossroads, faces pointing to every turn.

Sutra 6

If you say he is right, he will turn the other way, and you'll wonder why you're feeling as if left.

Sutra 7

If you say he is left, then it would not be wrong to wonder what happened when you were right.

Sutra 8

If you say he enters, he will rush out, like your eyes from your face, into the ribs of who you love.

Sutra 9

If you say he goes out, he will, like the one cut by your glance, want admittance to your In Ward.

Sutra 10

If you say, this way, be sure he'll be that way, if you say that's fine, too, he will say I like it this way.

Sutra 11

If you say, come, he'll go, if you say go, he'll spread his mat right in your heart, and shut the door.

Sutra 12

When it's Skanda, the Lord of Kataragama, it's better not to say where, for he wants every *where*.

Sutra addressed to women

Warnings: Sutra 1–4

Sutra 1

Be warned: he will lean so his breath can jostle the script off your forehead.

Sutra 2

Beware: he'll politely mop your brow & all your mother said to remember.

Sutra 3

Beware: his artful comments'll make your willing heart desert you for him.

Sutra 4

Be well-warned: this is a lifetime thing: you say *Yes* to him and it's for*ever*.

Assurances: Sutra 5–8

Sutra 5

Be assured: when he presides in the poets' assembly, he gives up his tricks.

Sutra 6

Be assured: the tests to measure craft and skill are not harsher for women.

Sutra 7

Be assured: you'll get no embarrassing concessions because you're female.

Sutra 8

Be assured: he has already loved several keen women, as poets, not lovers.

Instructions: Sutra 9–12

Sutra 9

Go turn into a roll of carpets, for he will surely decide to procession himself.

Sutra 10

Become cutlass-sharp, for he will become thickets, tangled and unyielding.

Sutra 11

Become caisson-firm for when he decides to be a well, wobbly & caving in.

Sutra 12

Know that the world is illusion; he blinks – it goes; go dissolve into his eyes.

Skanda, Lord of Kataragama, is faultlessly faithful to poets and women: to be both is a bonus.

Sutra of dhrupad

Sutra 1

To speak of him, like to sing dhrupad, forget the three worlds

Sutra 2

retire the guards, fill up the moats, let down the drawbridges

Sutra 3

take down the flags and the pennants; scratch out the blazon

Sutra 4

send all your trumpets, clarinets, horns and drums to auction

Sutra 5

chamberlains, stewards & heralds, send them to vigil corpses

Sutra 6

give up your chariots, your sceptre and crown; exile yourself

Sutra 7

become the cup put out to catch the drip from glooming skies

Sutra 8

be the clever cook they lend out to neighbouring kingdoms

Sutra 9

go witness matchless Ravana strumming his innards for god

Sutra 10

turn into the one that sets her hand over her chest & says no

Sutra 11

shut your eyes and leap off cliffs, where the ancient rocks lie

Sutra 12

strum your tanpura and strip the notes of their many guises.

To speak of Lord Skanda of Kataragama, like to sing dhrupad, is to be sound.

Sutra of beasts and birds

Sutra 1

Say not among beasts he is the taciturn lion, for he is the ant awaiting sweet.

Sutra 2

Say not among birds he is the soaring eagle, for he is the parrot awaiting talk.

Sutra 3

Say not he is the useful elephant, for he is the cat scurrying to lap.

Sutra 4

Say not he is the fluttering rain bird, for he is the vulture sitting still.

Sutra 5

Say not he rations like the hardy camel, for he is the always-thirsting dog.

Sutra 6

Say not he is the white swan, for he is the peacock, emerald and more.

Sutra 7

Say not he is that fearsome tiger, for he is this mute ox, fielding crops.

Sutra 8

Say not he is the brooding roof owl, for he's the raucous calling cuckoo.

Sutra 9

Say not he is the loose monkey, for he is the faithful carrier pigeon.

Sutra 10

Say not he is barnyard fowl, for he is departing southerly birds.

Sutra 11

Say not he is the retreating centipede, for he is the leech that doesn't fall.

Sutra 12

Say not he is the faraway ocean, for he is this new rain running all over.

Sutra 13

Say not he is the elusive hawk, for he is the practiced wrist that birds want.

Say the right thing and Lord Skanda of Kataragama may stop changing shapes.

Sutra of the five elements

Mud

Sutra 1

Know that Skanda is the mud in which this world roots and branches;

Sutra 2

like red mud mixes in rain-wet to form soil, the world mixes in him;

Sutra 3

become like mud, grain & every grain calling him to come and mix;

Sutra 4

become like fields & like plains, like forests of mud waiting for rain.

Wet

Sutra 1

Know that Skanda is the rain in which this world washes and rinses;

Sutra 2

like monsoon bathes hills and mountaintops, the world soaks in him;

Sutra 3

become like steep slopes that he may run down to wait in the plains;

Sutra 4

become like hillocks & knolls, like valleys of rain-wet awaiting warm.

Warm

Sutra 1

Know that Skanda is the warm in which this world heats and thaws;

Sutra 2

like winter fires warm our crops and cattle, the world basks in him;

Sutra 3

become like dried kindling that he may catch against you and flame;

Sutra 4

become like twigs, like tinder logs, mouths of flame, waiting for air.

Air

Sutra 1

Know that Skanda is the air in which this world surges and billows;

Sutra 2

like swift winds lift up prayer flags on hills, the world flaps in him;

Sutra 3

become like gossamer pennants so he may rush into you and heave;

Sutra 4

become like ribbons, like banners, like all airborne things seeking sky.

Sky

Sutra 1

Know that Skanda is the dark sky in which this world clouds & breaks;

Sutra 2

like seeding waters collect around specks, this world gathers in him;

Sutra 3

become like dense clouds so that he may converge in you and pour;

Sutra 4

become like drops of water, like clouds waiting to fall and mix in mud.

Lord Skanda is all: be plants when he is mud; be mud when he is rain; be winged seeds when he is wind; be sun when he is sky and when he is he, you can be you.

Sutra of the fierce tiger

Sutra 1

Know that he is like the fierce tiger: forest, swamp & rocky hills are his hangouts.

Sutra 2

Know that he is like the fierce tiger: bristle, thorn and bramble are his bedding.

Sutra 3

Know that he is like the fierce tiger: dark nights dodge the lantern of his eyes.

Sutra 4

Know that he is like the fierce tiger: sunny days court the yellow of his stripes.

Sutra 5

Know that he is like the fierce tiger: dutiful census-takers want a tracker on him.

Sutra 6

Know that he is like the fierce tiger: resolute photographers want a frame of him.

Sutra 7

Know that he is like the fierce tiger: persistent hunters are warned of his ways.

Sutra 8

Know that he is like the fierce tiger: ambitious writers are cued in on his deeds.

Sutra 9

Know that he is like the fierce tiger: safari groups hope to get a glimpse of him.

Sutra 10

Know that he is like the fierce tiger: wildlife guides try and be the first to sight him.

Sutra 11

Know that he is like the fierce tiger: his fame precedes him, scaring some, luring some.

Sutra 12

Know that Skanda of Kataragama is like the fierce tiger: master of this forest we call the world.

Sutra of the sky

Sutra 1

Do not say he's smelted gold in morning skies, for he's ingots of silver by night.

Sutra 2

Do not say he is halogen-glare in midday skies, for he's lamp-dull at gloaming.

Sutra 3

Do not say he's rain-rich skies over Mawsynram, for he's wind-robbed in Jaisalmer.

Sutra 4

Do not say he's full-moon's-orb-white skies, for he's star-sprinkled in the last quarter.

Sutra 5

Do not say he's weepy lovers' skies of stratus, for he's banners of wedding-red altocumulus.

Sutra 6

Do not say he's the skyway for passing birds, for he roofs Sholicola and Montecinla habitats.

Sutra 7

Do not say he is the sky that runs from fields of dying crop, for he's the one that stops to weep.

Sutra 8

Do not say he's the sky rolling in from the south-west, for he's the one that clouds from NE, too.

Sutra 9

Do not say he is the bland sky peacocks refuse, for he's well spiced with thunder and lightning.

Sutra 10

Do not say he's the sky that rouses singers' voices, for he's the one that lullabies poets' words.

Sutra 11

Do not say you can't say what sky he is, for he waits, so your words may root, sprout, leaf & branch.

Sutra 12

Say that all skies are Skanda, Lord of Kataragama, who clouds & bursts to irrigate our poetry's crop.

Sutra of refusal

Sutra 1
Refuse, if he offers you a seat beside him.

Sutra 2
Refuse, if he offers you a work-day off.

Sutra 3
Refuse, if he offers his indigo shawl as cover from rain.

Sutra 4
Refuse, if he asks you to pick a theme for your poem.

Sutra 5
Refuse, if he stops mid-work to ask if you'd like to eat.

Sutra 6
For he wants to be unthroned when you stand reciting.

Sutra 7

For he's given those days, the promise of your poetry.

Sutra 8

For he's checking if you know you can turn into a peacock when he's near.

Sutra 9

For he's checking if you've understood that he alone is your theme.

Sutra 10

For he's checking if you know your poetry can quell hunger: his & yours.

Sutra 11

While you wait, teach yourself to say No and again No, and then, again, No.

Sutra 12

For this is Skanda of Kataragama, who wants you to refuse all but poetry and him.

THE BECAUSE OF EVERY WHY

Guide Poems

The 5 Ws and 1 H

When you've finished – after you're re-worked, edited and saved, that's when he'll strike. His weapons are silent and deadly, and in an instant your carefully built poem and everything in it will be gone: rows of streets, townships and citadels, all your ports and libraries – they will be nothing but dust. And you will be standing in a field of waste. That's when you'll know you should've asked him to lead you through the lines to that last full-stop, marking when you've finished.

'What have you finished?' he'll ask, examining what you've done. He'll smile and walk around the poem you sweated over. He might ask, 'What can it do? Will it roll along the riverbank's uneven? Can it stand in water? Will it run with blowing wind? Can it hold when I charge into battle?' Then he'll take the front wheel of your metaphor and give it such a shake, the thing will come off in his hands. At this, he will look surprised and ask, 'What! Did you not say you have finished?'

Where you finish, that's where he'll want to begin. He'll position himself at the last and march towards the first. On the way, he might grab the pen you laid down, and run it through your cavalry of words. Or he might encircle and hold them. Or run the pen diagonally across your page, cutting off all negotiation. On a rare day, he might explain where your strategies failed, and show you what to do in order to ensure that nothing can say your endings are better off elsewhere.

Why finish at all, you'll ask yourself. Why not just call it work-in-progress? Why does he decide that you're done or not? It's not as if he does anything to help you finish, in fact he does everything to hold you up, asking, 'Why this? Why that? Why not that other or this other?' You'll ask yourself why answers are so clear when he's not standing in front of you, but go up in smoke when he leans over and says to you, 'Why do you feel it's finished? Why, this is no finish at all.'

Who finishes, only they can read in the great assembly, you know that. But who's to help you finish? See! Who looks at you, watching slyly, as your head begins to whirl? Who makes your words run off, as if by a spell, whenever he is near? He is the one who holds the rights to the alphabets; it is he who owns the grammars. It is he who will riddle you with his deceptive question: 'Who are you? Do I know you?' Remember, the only right retort to this: My Lord, are you He who finishes?

How will you ever finish? How will you plant images in your poem, when he is constantly running amok through the fields? How are you going to build on the metaphors when he routinely shakes them loose? Don't worry that you will not find answers to these problems and make it to the assembly, for let me tell you, I know he is the *because* of every 'Why?' the *here* of every 'Where?'. And it is he who becomes the *now* to every single 'When?'. He is always *how* you will finish. This is Skanda, Kataragama's Lord, who apprentices and masters poets, waiting and watching till the finish.

Road map

Part One: Preparation

Stand here, look at the holy hill, raring up like a serpent, its hood spread;
stand till it uncoils and strikes; count out your doubts, then climb the hill.

At this climb's start, counting offerings, there he is, the jumbo-faced god;
at his will, our paths could turn into dead ends, and our progress up, stop.

Without a stop here, you will not locate signboards or milestones en route;
without his permits, nothing journeys – he holds the tolls for all our ways.

Travel after paying levy to this god or the roads will dissolve into mirages;
travelling towards our hill-god, we wait for the elephant-head to nod *okay*.

You must know that he's a stickler who will triple-check every document;
you must also know that he's kind, for he's the Lord & Lifter of Obstacles.

Pray he doesn't turn your going into an obstacle course, beware, always;
pray well, so he keeps your maps and compass steadfast and you, aware.

Part Two: First encounter with the god of our hill
Beware, you'll perish if you go unprepared to meet the sly god of our hill;
beware his mindfulness test: he'll get in your mind and erase everything.

He may ask you to give up everything for a single word; even, just a letter;
he may want more, so teach your face to not look so desperate and willing.

When he's wilful, go ask his mother's help – the mother of this & all worlds;
when she asks what you want, tell her to give what she will, for she is kind.

The games he plays most often are hide-and-seek & who's-as-strong-as-me;
the fact that you're new at this will not exempt you from his endless tricks.

Novices mistakenly think he means what he says and will play by the rules;
novices believe he's trusty because he smiles and invites them to his home.

Home is where the heart is; he will take your heart up to his hilltop home;
home here, he'll say, but remember, the home you seek is for your poems.

Part Three: What he wants

He wants you to chase him, and the chase to be a tale recounted long after;
he wants you to go round the bend, but keep your poem sound in sense.

Sentenced to this and other lives, all you can do is ask that he go with you;
sentences and what they say will determine whether you're worth his time.

Before you ask, remember that everything in the universe is in his employ;
before time can skip, catch it by the hand and stop it, till you have spoken.

Know that when he comes, his faces turned to six sides, your words'll rebel;
know that your language will mutiny, all your tenses and punctuation, too.

All your un-ranked verses will charge to his citadel, to enlist in his armies;
all your best troops will assemble under the rippling pennant of his face.

His deadpan look'll tell nothing: you'll never know when he ups the ante;
his grace is vast, though. He tricks but blesses – so learn to praise him well.

A poem of entreaty, to tell the Lord of Pazhani that the poet is feeling insecure

Skanda, Lord of Kataragama, here I am;
first light is only stirring in the east,
but I'm fully awake, ready to be written.
This morning, can you write me happy?

Happy are all things in this time; birds
stir to sound, dew shakes and falls,
and the poets wait for word from you.
Today, please write me without riddle.

Riddle the scape of the world, if you will;
only, let other people stumble, fall
and cry *Skanda* and make your lips smile.
This morning, write me without fall.

Fall and rise, is all the sun does every day,
forever, but he does not pall; let me
learn to track you in my falling and rising.
Can you write me with that function?

Function and appearance, just like
meaning and word, and She and He, are
the body & breath of all things, they say,
Please write me with that bond clear.

Clear your page, plough its hardpans,
furrows, ridges; scatter word and sense,
till, till evenly mixed, then write me in.
Will you write me in with robust roots?

Roots must be tough to make a good
crop, and the one who minds the field
should be very enthusiastic, it is said.
Write me with notes on these things.

Things come, and things go, they say,
but nothing stays forever and the trick,
they say, is to charm that nothing; so,
will you write me in with that spell?

Inside poets' hearts, your every visit
requires an assembly hall, and for your
followers, endless boarding and lodging.
So please, will you write me furbished?

Me, me, me, cry people, beasts, birds;
everyone wants to walk with you, but
I'd rather not make a fool of myself,
so, today, will you write me very silent?

Silent and still calling, I'm ready to be
written and edited, because I know you
don't read the way anyone else does,
so come, write me experimental today.

Today, tomorrow, yesterday, it goes
on and I want to be on a page with you
always, so come write me yourself, friend
to all poets, Skanda, Lord of Kataragama.

Guide poem (1)

They say that
there are times
when he will come,
his tiny ankleted
feet skipping on
the scratchy floor of
your meagre house,
taking care not to
step on the palm
leaves, inkpots, quills
and styluses, to lean
against you, where
you're seated, on
your worn grass mat.
They say he may
put his baby hands
on your shoulder
and press a loud
kiss on your cheek.
If your eyes fill, they
say, he will reach

his hand over,
brush your tears
away and say,
Silly poet. They say,
sometimes
he might climb
on your lap and ask
you to read to him
and when you're
done, he'll clap
his hands and laugh.
He may lean
against your chest,
sigh and fall asleep.
Sometimes,
once in a
thousand lives, he
may make dreams
like this come true:
that child god who
lives on Pazhani,
who can tell you
how to make a bad
poem, good.

Guide poem (2)

Remember
this: at some point, he's
going to get nervous,
thinking of his boast;
he'll start wondering
if his poets are really
the best, he'll begin
to fret that you don't
have what it takes,
and that's when he'll
start sending free
reading and
editing offers –
anonymously –
and let me tell you,
you'll be tempted.
But you've
got to say,
Lord
and beg him
not to

beg
you to be smarter than
you want to be.
You've got to
tell him
to let you make
your own ask.
Tell him you can't
need what he wants.
He's going to
tell everyone
how you've
been begging
him to grant you
inspiration,
(when all you've
been asking for is
to be left alone to
work)
and now,
when he wants to,
how you're being
stubborn.
That's because
he's hoping
popular opinion
will sway your
resolve.

He'll
coax and cajole,
he'll insist
and demand,
but you must say
that if you were
to ignore the
difference between
want & need,
you'll surely lose
your reputation
as a poet.
Assert yourself: do
what
you need to,
while you can still want to.

Of an incident that throws light on why they say poets must dress up when they visit Murugan

You're only going to
show your work,
they said to her,
why're you dressing up
like you're going to a wedding?
You'll make a fool of yourself,
they told her, but she paid no
heed: they weren't there,
the last time she had
gone to show him her work.

She had been wearing
work clothes; he had
looked at her, and nodded
a greeting, but when she went
closer, to hand him

the palm-leaf bundle, he, the Lord
of Pazhani, had whispered
to her, 'Bah! Poet's clothes?
Today, of all days, when
these out-of-town poets are here?'

His own clothes in indigo
silk – gold-silver-rainbow-colour
embroidered – and his turban
of crimson and gold, shimmered.
His waistband, his necklaces
and the many rings on his fingers
sparkled with gems: marakatam,
neelam, gomedakam, muthu,
manikyam, pavalam,
vaidooryam and more.

'Poets' clothes, really?' he had
snapped at her
and before she got back to her seat,
someone had
accidentally let slip an inkpot,
its indigo running all over her
white clothes, and then
he was calling out, loudly,
'Someone get her a change of
clothes; we can't have our
writers sitting in the assembly
dripping ink; however poetic

that may seem, it'll stain
the seats and the floor.'

Oh no!
She wasn't going to listen to
them: much better to over-dress,
and be laughed at, than
to have indigo breasts for weeks.

The Lord of Pazhani tests the crazy poet again, with his two wives present

Who,
he asks,
seated on top of that high hill
called Pazhani,
who are you going to pick?
Me? Or *him*?
That one you've foolishly
fallen in love with.

Lord,
she says,
standing beside his peacock,
emerald and blue,
I'm not going to pick either
you or him.

You must, he says,
I'm your god –
I insist.

I won't, she says,
I'm your poet –
I refuse.

Let's ask them,
he says,
pointing to his two wives.

Yes, let's ask them,
she says,
smiling at those clever ones.

The one on the left
says,
If I were you,
I'd choose love;
on the right, the other
says,
I would choose love,
if I were you.

Love, is it?
asks the poet.

Picking up her parchments
and stylus,
she clasps them to her
chest and turning to him
says,
Lord, I've chosen.

You've chosen well,
he says, a smile on his lips
and an inkhorn full
of his favourite
indigo ink
in the hand he's holding
out to her.
She smiles, relieved
that today her wits
didn't desert her;
his wives smile, relieved
that today he was okay
with clichés.

He smiles, thinking
of the
indigo-and-red saree he's
asked his weavers to make
for when she goes to
Madurai's temple, where
he will come to make
offerings –
that man she tried not
to fall in love with.

A monologue to show how poets' obstinate standing up to him, in the face of his accusations, pleases the god

Vela,
you're mean: just
because I spent more
time picking out the saree
for his housewarming – the
one I've lost my heart to –
than for my attendance at
your poetry reading, you
put all these obstacles in
my way?
How can you be like this?
I chose the white for you,
because you're a sanyasi,
and you did not look at the
pallu of this *shroud-white*
saree you're turning
your nose up at. It's called
mayuri – if you had looked

at it, you'd know why, but
why would you, you just
want to trouble me, no?

What!
I'm shameless, Vela? You're
the one with all the wives
and lovers. Stop it
Vela, I'm not courting him –
women don't court men;
men do the courting, and
anyway, he's not courting
me either, stop your
nonsense. You just stay
on the top of that hill;
don't bother coming down,
you've no idea how
civilised people live.
You can't just come down
and start talking about
sarees and courtship! And then
draw a tangent from there to
say I'm neglecting you.
You don't know anything about
sarees – your two wives
clearly have no dress sense,
they will wear anything they
are given. And you!
Abba! Your clothes could

light up a whole town's
darkness.

What? Go away, I'm tired of
you and your demands
and pranks, and tricks.
Take what? What's this?
What's in this bag, now?
A saree! Two sarees?
Identical? Indigo and green,
speckled with gold and pink.
Show off! I'm surprised there's
no tag that says 'Pazhani Mills'
or 'Pazhamudhircholai Silks'
or 'Sri Murugan Looms'.
Oh, this does have a label, let's
see what it says; 'Tenmozhi
Limited Edition Sarees'.

Where are you? Gone! Before
I can say anything. Pah! What a
god you are! Always, all the time,
you have the last word, no?

What his favourite poet said, when the novice poets asked her about dealing with the Lord of Pazhani

You're probably used to
patrons who practice
a minimum level of
propriety, but be
warned, not this one:
the Lord of Pazhani
knows no such restrictions.

When he's reading your
work, or he's struck
by an idea
he wants you to
execute, nothing will stop
him from getting you
started right away.

If it's raining,
he'll send you an umbrella;

if there's a road block,
he'll send his peacock to
fly you to him;
if you're off on a picnic, he'll
send showers to make you
scurry back home;
if you're making pickles,
or mending clothes,
or weaving mats,
or salting meats, he'll send
word to your mother, and she,
who said *you're neglecting*
your household duties,
will shoo you away, saying,
your brains
will rot if you don't use them,
go to work.

What if you're
with a man,
you might ask, will our
patron, the Lord of Pazhani,
be more circumspect?
Oh, my dear,
don't fool yourself; that'll
probably be the day
he decides the town-crier
is best suited
to the task of reminding
negligent poets

of their duties: you're
likely to have one at your
door, calling out the list
of your pending
commissions and
begging you to report
back to work immediately.

You may be conducting
an exam,
you may be attending a trial,
a magic show, a reading
by poets from all the lands
of our glorious south;
you may be at a naming
ceremony, a marriage, a funeral,
an alms-giving, a sanyasa
deeksha; you may be on the bank
of the Kaviri,
offering prayers for
the souls of your ancestors,
but if he wants you,
he'll do whatever will take
you to him right then.

Sometimes you'll go to
avoid further embarrassment,
sometimes you'll go
because you're afraid, and

sometimes you'll march there,
so angry you'll want to tell him
it's all over, but however it
happens, you'll see
that when he wants you there,
he'll have you there.

But when you have
your period, and you're
sticky and cramping, then
your mother will send
his messenger back – without
telling you.
She'll cross her arms across
her chest and say, 'No'.

And then what, you ask?
Will he leave you alone?

Oh no!
Then he will come to you,
he'll appear at the door
of your room, where you're
lying on the bed or leaning
against pillows
and ask if he may step in,
and you,
you'll know that a
No won't stop him, so you'll

be mute, angry tears
stinging your eyes,
your hands ready to pummel
him if he dares come
close enough; sharp words
straining against your tongue,
fighting to be unleashed.
And then? Then he'll lower
himself onto your bed, holding
out a vial of kashayam, and a
poultice that his clever hill-wife
has made, and you'll forget you
just swore you would have
nothing more to do with him.
With one hand rubbing your back,
he'll coax you to swallow the bitter;
then he'll go to your kitchen and
return with the heated poultice,
which he'll press to your belly
with such practiced ease,
you'll forget your mother
said that on these days,
only she may touch you.

In a while,
the potion will uncurl
your insides and straighten your
back. The press
of his knowing fingers

against your spine will rouse
the breath inside your lungs;
your lips'll twitch, to think how
your words brought him
down
from his high hill, leaving
work – and play – to wait on you,
and that's when you'll hear
his voice saying,
'Time to stop being a baby,
let's get to work.'

A poem to show how sometimes, the god could save himself some trouble, if there was a guide poem for him

They: the god's two wives

Valli smiled;
Deva did not smile.
She said, 'Valli, look at
the poet's sore neck, her
bending back and her
stooping shoulders – see
how that makes her
rib cage close up – there's not
enough room there for all
three of us; do you think
the Lord of Pazhani is
glad that her chest is
caving in,
leaving just enough
space for him alone?'
He was smiling,

the god, their husband,
as if he was hearing
an old wives' tale.

she: the poet

Deva and Valli
went to the
poet in dream;
they said:
build your core,
muscle up, make space
for us in your chest, we
want to live there, too,
with him, the one you call
Vela, and Friend,
for we love him, the way
you love that one – the
one you have fallen
in love with. The god
was smiling, still,
as if his wives
were being silly.

He: the poet's god

He was her god, and
she, his poet, so of
course, it was expected that he
worry when she got frail, and

weak. But when there was
just enough space for only he,
in her chest, he couldn't
help smiling: no one else
but he.
Then it occurred to him
that he would get lonesome
for his wives, the two clever women
whom he adored, and she, his poet,
would pine for that man,
the one she had tried so hard
not to fall in love with.
And then, she would not write.
That made him stop smiling,
and he too went and stood
behind his two wives
in the poet's dream,
nodding seriously when
they said to her: work on
your core, build up your chest.

SHAKE YOUR WINGS, FLY TO HIM

Messages

Collaboration

My dear parrot,
take pity on me, wake up,
shake your wings, fly to him, who left,
ripping my heart up by its roots;
go tell him of my pitiable state.
Tell him monsoon greens the hills,
for in this rain, all growing
things put out shoots, only
my heart neither sprouts nor leafs.

When you fly over orchards
filled with flowering trees, you might
look down and see him on a
flower-decked swing, with another
woman, but
don't hesitate to tell me. I know
these things happen, I am no fool.

When you reach his city,
hemmed by leaping waves, you might
look down and see him in a
canopied boat, rowing with another
woman, but

don't hesitate to tell me. I know
these things happen, I am no fool.

When you reach his home,
filled with happy people, you might
fly inside and see him on a
plush bed, sporting with another
woman, but
don't hesitate to tell me. I know
these things happen, I am no fool.

Dear parrot, remember
this: when you reach the home
of my Lord of Pazhani,
with the overflowing word-stores,
if you see him at his desk,
composing a poem, with another
woman,
for pity's sake, when you fly back,
stop yourself from telling me.
I am no fool, I know
that writing doesn't just happen.

Action & dialogue

Dear parrot,
will you turn away from
that pomegranate for a moment?
Can't you see the state I am in?
Come and tell me how to
send a message to the Lord
of Pazhani, the one they call
Mutthukumaran,
that cruel man who has
left me and gone,
they say,
to a woman more suitable
than I.
Who's going to tell him
how miserable I am?
Dear parrot, don't you
have friends among
those noisy peacocks
that live on Pazhani hill,
who, they say,
he tells his secrets to?
Can't you find out
from one of them,

what he's doing
and what he intends?
If you tell them how
cruel he's been to me,
won't their hearts melt?
Won't it loosen
their tongues?
Tell them how it was
he who came to me, and
then wanted to stay.
Tell them about how
he wanted to see me,
all the time –
how he would sulk
if I didn't want to
pillow my face on
his chest, or if I wanted
to take my arms
from around his neck.
Ask them, dear parrot,
if it's fair that
now he can't seem to
remember anything?
Tell those peacocks to
tell him how the women
mock me, saying,
he's left me for one
who doesn't waste her time
reading and writing – because
it's action he wants, not dialogue.

I have nothing to say to that
because I've seen things
they haven't;
when he presses his lips
to mine, his eyes don't shut,
as they should,
if tasting honey
is all he wanted,
but instead,
stay open and widen,
when his lips feel
the salt and tang
of new words.
And when my limbs
grip his waist,
drawing him deeper in,
why does he bring his
ear to my head,
as if he's listening
to a voice he knows?
Why, even through the
daze of coupling, I know that
he takes my fingers –
busy on his reddening face,
his dark chest,
his unguarded waist –
to his lips,
to kiss their ink stains.
Dear parrot, fly to him
and tell him,

I'm not taken in by
all this gossip, tell him,
I know he wants me
to beg.
Tell him I know what
that does to him
(and to me).
Tell him, I beg,
beg him to come back.
Tell him, I've
laid out new sheets
of paper, and the
Venetian-glass vials
at my bedside are full
with intoxicating inks.
Tell him about
my new tutor,
from across the
seas, in whose language
I have been practicing
to say: *Lord of Pazhani,*
Mutthukumaran,
mahagani-dark, kurinji-
sweet, whose reading
is a prize that can make
the most inventive of
poets in all of great
Tamizhagam
out-write herself.
He knows where I

am: if his lips haven't
got calloused and dull
from all the action, then
he can try and coax the
words out of my mouth.
Tell him I'm not fooled
by any of this;
I know the secret those
women don't:
for the likes of him,
there is little thrill
in action without dialogue.

Learn your craft, they said

My Lord of High Hills,
you who rule in Pazhani
and whose rules of
writing are yet to be bested,
please read this through
and if it moves you,
come back to me.
I can no longer
look anyone in the eye
for fear they will see
I've a man in my heart;
I can't sleep because
as soon as I do,
you're knocking to be
let out of my dream;
I can't eat, for every time
I raise food to my mouth,
it seems you're at my side,
wanting a kiss.

What's to be said,
everything's become
about you; even my hair

refuses to fall on
this pillow, now that
your head is not on it.

Lord of Pazhani,
what have you done?
I tell myself
if I write poems
without you in them,
I'll be fine, but
as soon as I
begin to write,
you worm, storm
or charm your way in.

I don't know
what to do with you,
but I know, even less,
what to do without you:
I wish they'd taught me
all this during my
apprenticeship,
but apprentices are
taught to believe in
craft, and not in a
god of poetry.

Footnotes

Dear friend,
come help me draft this letter
to he who has left me,
they say, for another;
I want to stay dignified,
make no mention of the past,
just ask him what he means
to do now and leave it at that –
but that setting sun makes me lose
my senses; I weep remembering the round
of my teeth on his shoulder,
the first time he joined with me,
and how spreading tulasi and aloe,
my fingers slowed, making
his brown eyes gleam.

Dear friend,
I want to quietly tell him
that I am not the type to
stand in the way of a man's
desire for another woman,
I want to stay composed and
make no mention of the past,

just ask him what he wants
of me now and leave it at that –
but those summer bees make me lose
my mind; I weep remembering the buzz
of his voice in my ears every time
he joined with me, saying,
you're mine, you're mine.

Oh, my dear,
there's no hope of my
being able to write this
with any decorum or dignity,
just take this quill and this ink
from me, and write to him,
the Lord of Pazhani,
tell him of my plight, beg him,
plead with him, cajole him,
promise him grand kirtanams,
racy javalis, delicate padams,
offer clever pallavis that play
with his name and fame;
offer gardens full of flowers,
and bees making honey
as sweet as poetry.
Promise him my life:
all my manuscripts, my inks,
pens, my lexicons,
collected over long years.

My friend,
how can he forget that in all these
lands, he's not found anyone
who can work with the fire in his lines,
the lusty thrust of his similes,
or the urgent
impel in his metaphors, like I do? How
can he forget the poems we started
together?
I wish I could stay dignified, make no
mention of the happy past
or of my hopes for the future, but
when I think of him, past and present
and unformed future run onto
my page like dense text and
everything else but he, seems like
a gratuitous footnote.

No need to take refuge in prose

My dear friend,
what is that
sound?
Tell me, is it he?
Has he
taken pity
and returned to me?

Quick, sit me
up now, gently,
for every inch
of me
hurts from lying
down so long.

Unlatch
the doors, open
the windows,
but wait,
rub some
colour on my
sallow cheeks.

Come now,
quickly, give me
a change of
clothes –
this white
will surely
scare him off.

Give me that
vial of vetiver,
the
kanmayi
and
kungumam,
but first,
give me
a drink of water.
For I want to
speak.

Bring the
yellow and pink
songbirds
back, let them
sing; release
the green
peacocks –
let them dance.
Quick,

sit me up, see
if I can stand;
it seems even
my bones
don't work
when he is gone.

My dear, is it he,
Pazhani's Lord?
Why do you look
at me like that?
Get a hold on myself?
Get a cure?

My friend,
there is no cure,
for there is
no one who can
delight me the way
he does:
how his chest
sings, when he draws
my face to it,
how his hands
tremble when they grip
the box of my ribs,
how his nostrils flare
when he hits the trail of
vetiver at my throat;

how his hands skip
over my belly and dart
past my hips to run up
the curve of my back;
how his eyes
shut when I pull him
into me. You don't know
the thrill of his lips
opening mine, his tongue
teasing, before he
presses into my mouth
a new word he's found.
You don't know
how it feels when
he begs me to say
what I want him to do,
in one of the languages
I'm learning. You
can't know what
it is I feel, when, as he
climaxes, I hear him
say my name over
and over and it is
the name I sign my
poems with.
The truth is,
dear friend, in all these
many worlds, he

alone
knows how to
address me, so that
I don't have to turn
to prose in order to
answer.

The gift

That wasn't him, was it, my dear? How my heart sinks,
no, don't look so crestfallen; enough of this weeping
and pining. Give me back my white robes, wipe my
face clean, release all those birds, let them go home
to tree hollows and crags and crannies. Find me a stout
stick, bring me a sword, ask the stablemate to prepare
me a swift horse. I will ride up the high mountains, far
higher than his hills; tell the Lord of Pazhani I am done
with longing and waiting. I'm going up the mountain,
far away from my home, and his, to snow and wind;
I will stand on cliffs at moonrise, and at dawn I will
pull off my robes and dive into that river's swirl and
float with leaves, fish and shadows cast by the rising
sun. I will lie under the sun's first light and warm my
breath, gone frail from all this weeping and wailing.
I will teach my skin not to wait for his touch. I will eat
wild things, say wild things, and watch wild creatures
hunt and mate, I will let the fierce moon bring tears to
my eyes, when she rises and sets. I will spend my days
with wind, earth, sun, water, and all the space I want.

He has sent word? What does the good Lord of Pazhani
want? A parting gift? What could I possibly want from

him? He has nothing that I don't have, nothing he can give me: I have palaces that match his in grandeur and size, I have wealth and finery, servants by the score, my libraries are stocked with books he may have never even seen, in my retinue are dancers and singers to out beat his, I can best him in any debate, I can draw crowds to my readings, I am good-looking – if, when he enters a room, heads turn, watch what happens when I come in through any door! Tell the Lord of Pazhani, once mine, as he repeatedly said, who gladdened my heart and my body, that there is nothing he has that I don't, or rather the only thing he has, more valuable than all else in this world, is me. And that, I don't need his permission to take. But tell him this: when I go, with me will go all my words, and that, he will have a great deal of trouble replacing.

What the queen says to her divan, when he returns without an audience with the Lord of Pazhani

My dear sir,
what do you mean, you couldn't
get an appointment? How could you
be refused an appointment?
You are divan to one of
the mightiest kingdoms this side of
the Vindhyas, one as large and
as powerful as theirs.
They said no, and you just came back?
Can't you see the state I am in? Isn't
it your responsibility to ensure your
sovereign's wellbeing?
Protocol allows only you such
intimacy in my life, but what's the use,
it's as if you're blind. You have seen

me since my birth, but you can't
see the state I am in now?

Ever since I met *him* at the
Seunas' banquet, a month ago,
and he promised to visit me here,
I have not been able to do my job
as the ruler of this kingdom: it's days
since I went on a night
watch, or duelled. I have stayed
away from grievance
meetings, for I'm unsure of
my judgment.
My poor horse stands
at my window,
looking towards the hills, but all
I can do is let her eat jaggery from my
hand and put my face on hers,
then my tears run into her
eyes, making her toss her head.

Yes, sir, I know all the things
you're going to say now, about
how *able* I am: you're going to
remind me of my gifts of
judgment and
my skill as a warrior,
but my dear divan,
all that

was before I met him.
When he looked at me,
I forgot every skill I have ever learned
and I could do nothing to dodge the
arrows of his eyes, piercing
the armour of my ribs and striking my heart.
But in truth, when he touched my hand
and turned his eyes on me, all I
knew was, I was glad to be a woman;
all I wanted was to be wounded
and for him to bend and lift me up in
his arms and balm my wounds with…
Oh, dear sir, see how my tongue runs
away with itself,
I am not myself, sir
I am not myself, don't you see what
I mean?

Ever since that birthday banquet,
when Seuna Singhana introduced me
to him, saying, 'This is the Lord of
mighty Pazhani, the warrior that
brave fighters long to duel with,
the patron that poets vie to write for,
husband to the great scholar Teivanai
and the brilliant warrior, Valli',
I have forgotten
how to be sovereign,

how to rule your kingdom;
how to read, how to hunt,
how to be myself – even
the things they said are in my
blood have run off.
All I want now is to be defeated
and taken captive
by the irresistible Mutthukumaran,
who loves like no other, and
on whose tongue my name
sounds as if he just invented it – he
who rides the emerald peacock,
lives on beauteous Pazhani hill,
and the quiver of
whose speech is always full.

She later apologises to her divan, and tells him what she would like done

Dear sir,
I beg your forgiveness
for my thoughtless speech
last evening: as you
saw, I was not quite myself.
I have decided to go to
Asan, at Edappadi –
yes, sir, the bodyguards
go with me, as will the
physician. I have sent word
to Asan, and he will have the
kalari readied for me: I am
going into training, for a
week. He has sent for the
archers and wrestlers
from Nellai, who
trained me during
my apprenticeship.
For the sword, and lance,

there is no one better in
all Tamizhagam than
Asan himself, as you know.

I will also work on the
incomplete manuscript of
one hundred verses to the
kind goddess of Kanchi,
which I have not
found the time and focus
to complete.
I believe it will ground
my thoughts and
strengthen my resolve
to win the one I love.

Sir, I know that the affairs
of state will go smoothly
under your supervision.
Yesterday, after you left,
I went around the town, on
a night ride, and today, I
met with the director of the
grievances cell and found, as
I had no doubt I would, that
there was nothing pending.

While I am away, I would
like you to do the following:

send word to the Lord of
Pazhani, invite him to a
competition, with me, to be
refereed by judges from both
our kingdoms: for the martial
rounds, his wife Valli on his side
and our friend, Singhana
of the Seunas, on ours;
for the arts, his first wife,
the scholar Teivanai
and our Asan.

Tell him that
we will duel for twice five
days, and these are the terms:
if I win – and we all know
I have as good a chance as
he – he will spend one week in
every month with me, in my
kingdom, in my palace,
in my, oh no! I'm not going to
let my tongue
run away with me again.
And should I lose,
and I know I can, if I let
myself,
then I will give up my stylus
and my parchments,
and never write a line again.

And he can have my entire library,
all my manuscripts, and all the
poets, scholars and songsters
in my retinue. Even our oracle,
if he so desires. Yes, sir,
I know those are the things I
have sworn to protect with my life.
But if I were to lose, we both know
there will be no life. Pray for me, sir,
pray that when I stand against him,
I don't forget how good I am at winning.

The divan updates her aunt about the duel between her niece and the Lord of Pazhani

Madam,
I write on behalf of
your departed
brother and his wife,
the parents of the child that was
left in my care, and who now
rules this great kingdom,
where the clouds and rivers
have never run dry, for we
have never run short of
rightness or poetry.

This is to inform you
that as agreed, she and the
Lord of Pazhani
competed, over ten long days.
The martial combats were
fierce: she and he both
sustained injuries that made

their trainers boast aloud
and thump their own chests.
The literary rounds were no
less thrilling: these were judged
by the Lord's wife, Teivanai,
and our Asan, and the
swordfight, archery, wrestling
and horseback jousting
by Valli, the Lord's other wife,
along with our neighbour,
valorous Singhana, the Seuna.

Archery went to Kumarayyan,
Pazhani's Lord, while in the
wrestling, she bested him, but
their javelins were equal, as
were their swords. As they tilted,
passed, lunged, feinted, fell,
picked themselves up and
parried again and again,
neither combatant seemed
able to beat the other,
and we feared it would
just go on and on till they
collapsed, but
then we saw Valli turn to
Singhana and exchange a few
words, then she stood up,
quoted the appropriate

reference, forbade further
physical combat, fixed
a time for versing, riddling
and storying, and called for
two days of rest.

The masseurs
and healers had their work
cut out for them, we were told,
but then, on the assigned
day and time, when the two appeared,
their wounds were invisible and
their faces incandescent, unsmiling.

What can I say about the competition?

There was never a moment when
we could pause and take stock:
their speech parried, tilted, passed,
stood up and parried again and again,
and it seemed neither could beat the
other, but in the end, it was your niece
that won: she was able to make up
a word from both his and her names,
to mean 'an equal opponent',
but he was unable to dismantle it
and make the opposite, which was the
condition, and when she did it,
with that untrammelled laugh we know

so well, the entire assembly stood, as
one, calling and clapping. There were
times when he seemed a little
distracted, but she was not
at all. That morning, when she stood
in the library, her hands running
over the parchments and scrolls, she
stopped at the one that had
the Tathagatha's sermon on nature
written in elegant Telugu
by Draksharama Shastrigaru, and
a shudder ran through her body;
when she straightened, drawing
her back straight and her waist as
taut as on the battlefield,
I think I knew things would
go in her favour.

When it was clear she had won,
the Lord of Pazhani praised her
in couplets that
rang and resounded,
bringing tears to many eyes,
including mine. He has
promised to return in three
weeks, when Rohini once more
shines at her brightest, to join
your niece, our queen, in secure
matrimony.

I write now to intimate you that all
arrangements have been taken care
of, and we await your arrival,
to hold the blessing ceremony
before sending out invitations.
Singhana Seuna has arrived, with
his retinue, and is doing all that a
brother would have done for your
niece. He himself will go to the
Big Three, with the wedding invite.

I remain, as always, sincerely,
a caretaker to this great kingdom,
now ruled by one as strong, wise
and righteous
as the one who ruled before her –
your brother, my dearest friend.

What Mutthukumaran said to his peacock, when it came back without a reply from Teivanai

You've come back again without a
reply to my message? What
do you mean, she didn't see you?
How can anyone
not see a peacock? And your voice
is so loud, it could wake a stone.
What do you mean, I should
give it up? As if you know anything.
The only thing you know is how
to spread your wings and preen.
People would think you're the god
and I'm your vehicle; maybe
they should say, *'There goes Paravani,*
the mighty peacock, and that's his vehicle,
the steadfast Mutthukumaran,
once the Lord of Pazhani.'

If only I had someone who would
do my bidding sincerely – I'm sure you

went there and when you saw her
and her friends,
you forgot my message and
decided to show off: you must have
shaken out your feathers and gone
for it in full style.
If only I had a trusty rat for a vehicle,
or a devoted lion, someone who's
not distracted by his own good looks.
No, don't say anything more,
I'll go find someone else
to deliver my messages – I'm a god,
remember,
they call me *Mutthukumaran*,
the one whose charm is unfailing.

Also what he said to his peacock, about not bringing a reply to his messages from Teivanai

Again? Empty-handed? Are
you sure you're
trying hard enough?
Tell me one thing:
is this your way
of teaching
me a lesson for saying
I would prefer brother's
rat or mother's lion
for
a vehicle?
Or,
and now be honest,
is it that you know
she doesn't care for me
and you're trying
to spare my feelings?
If that's the case,
you should just

tell me
so that I don't make
any more of
a fool of myself.

You're the only one who can tell me, to
my six faces, when I'm being foolish.

Yesterday,
in the poets'
assembly,
when Nakkeerar
pulled me up for
not being attentive,
you know what
happened?
That Madurai poet
was reading his new
poem series, I was
meant to listen
really carefully,
because he usually
gets the rhythm
just a little bit off,
but at some point,
my mind went to the
time Teivanai
visited us, with
her parents;

she'd asked Father
how Bharata's work
was going, you
know, with
his Natyashastra.
Father read out
parts of the chapter
on rhythm. Then, she
had a doubt and Father
took out his udukkai
and, tapping it, showed
her how the progression
of the beat cycle works,
only if you mentally
count what we call the
'unheard thought-beat'
which neither sound nor
sense will indicate.
It was only when
Nakkeerar glared
at me and said, 'Go
learn to count', that
I realised I had missed
a flaw in timing in
the Madurai poet's
poem.

You're the only one who tells me, to
my six faces, when I'm being foolish.

They tell me she comes to
the poets' assembly
only to hear me, but
when I begin to speak,
she looks bored. Yet she's
attentive enough,
smiling at the good lines
and not letting flaws
go by without a frown.
But wait! Can there be
truth in what they
say? Didn't she change
her nose pin from
ruby-red to ink-blue?
And of late, she's been
looking like
a piece of the sky,
for her
usual upper cloth of
gold-threaded white
is gone and in its place is
blue, lined with silver.
What do you mean, how
is that relevant? Don't
you remember she
was there when
our Madurai poet sang
of my love for indigo?

You're the only one who tells me, to
my six faces, when I'm being foolish.

You know the ways of
women,
my friend,
you've seen all the worlds;
tell me,
what does this mean?
If you think there's
no chance of her
caring for me,
you should just
tell me
so that I don't make
any more of
a fool of myself.
I will stop thinking of
her and concentrate on
my poets,
who wait on me,
saying,
'Mutthukumarayya,
you who know the fate
of all things, tell us what
to make of our words.'

I can't do this without you; you're the only
one who knows when I'm being foolish.

What the peacock said to himself, when Teivanai refused Murugan's note once again

Dear god, give me patience
– no, not my real god,
the love-sick Mutthukumaran –
some other god, his father or
uncle, perhaps,
oh, but they're just as bad.
Is there no one that's
level-headed,
not prone to bouts of
fancy that make them silly
beyond reason?
I should call on his mother,
the mother of all the worlds,
for She's really the only one who
can keep things in perspective.

Again and again, this
Kumarayyan, Lord in Pazhani,
God of Tamizh, he sends me

with notes to her, whose
father is king in the
kingdom of the gods,
and she,
known in all the worlds
for her scholarship and her kinship
with all creatures, how she
pretends not to see me
or hear my voice, which is so
loud, it could wake up a stone.

How trying this is for me,
going back and forth
between them. I don't
understand why he's being
so coy; in the past, he's always
been so forthright, but you
can't blame him – she's like
no one else,
he's nervous about every
word he writes to her –
I've seen him check and
double-check the rhymes
and the time measures
in the poems he sends her.

And she's so in love
with him, she changed
her nose pin from red to blue,

and her upper cloth from
gold-bordered-white to
indigo and silver,
after she heard
that poet from Madurai
sing of Kumarayyan's
love for blue.

God knows how long
they will keep this up –
my patience is running
out,
but I must admit, sometimes
even I'm moved by
how sweet they are:
he sits where she must pass
and then says,
See! She came this way
just to see me;
and she,
when she sits in the poets'
assembly, over which he
presides, she's lost to
the world, it's her friends
who are keeping tabs –
I've seen them whisper
to her to
'smile' or 'frown'
according to when the poets'

lines are good or bad.
And when he speaks,
on either side of her,
they hold her hands, to
keep her from clapping
every time he
opens his mouth.
The poor boy thinks
she's bored with what
he's saying, and has begun
to pore over old texts
to find new things to say.

I feel sorry for him, he's
never had to try so hard
before – for he's a
charmer consummate, and
his looks could turn anyone's
head, but more than all
that, it's always been his words,
they're like the honey that
nestles inside dew-beaded
flowers at daybreak,
and no one would consider
resisting them, for he's after all
Mutthukumaran, the best poet
in all the worlds, the only one
who knows how words will
turn out, every time.

Oh, there he goes again,
another note! Dear Mother, grant
me more patience.

Teivanai's answer to her friends, when they tell her to watch out

Don't tell me it's an accident he's wearing wild flowers and
eating figs that grow only on that hill, I'm no fool, you know.

Ever since he went to that hill, he's been unlike himself, he
no longer sleeps on mattresses and can't seem to bear the
touch of silk. He seems to have forgotten his love of poetry
and his lust for duels with lance, spear & twin-faced swords.

Don't tell me it's an accident he's doing all this. I'm no fool.

You say, 'set things right', but have you seen him jump from
sleep, to stand at the window, sighing? Have you blushed in

shame when his mother asks why you're letting him go off to
bathe in hill streams while his scented bath water goes cold?

Don't tell me it's an accident he's doing all this. I'm no fool.

They tell me the hunter's daughter has arms taut and strong,
they tell me she wears red flowers and her lips are as dark
as the figs he loves, he who is so enamoured of me, this
peacock-rider, owner of six and many more magnificent hills.

Dear friends, it's no accident he wears flowers and eats figs
from her hill; I am no fool and neither is she: we both know
that his love is unstoppable, so stop telling me it's an accident
he's doing all this. I'm no fool and never have been, you see.

Teivanai's answer to her friends when they tell her she's too trusting

*I hear they say that when he wanted to see my
best waistband, yesterday, I suspected nothing.*

Yesterday, when he returned from that hill at
dusk, worn out, why did I not guess, they ask,
at least when his peacock refused to meet my
eyes, should I not have known? They say they
thought it might come to this.

I hear they say that I never suspected anything.

My friends and cousins scold me, they whisper,
watch out. They said, he's called Guha, the one
who lives in the heart, and the word out there
is – he's always looking for new hearts to visit,
but I, they say, was too trusting.

I hear they say that I never suspected anything.

I am told her waist shimmers and bells ring as
she walks, Valli, the kurati. I'm told that when
he crosses her path, they swap knowing smiles.
And now my friends are saying my waistband's
missing – the one with gold bells.

How do they say that I didn't suspect anything,
when her face spreads wings and dances (like
mine), whenever he's near, and his eyes follow
her (like they follow me). The truth is, she and
I and he know that love for him is unstoppable.

Mutthukumaran scolds his older brother, for not helping him in his courtship of Valli

What's the use of a
big brother
like you,
if you can't even
devise
a way to make
her,
the dark-as-moss
hunter girl
they call Valli,
look at me with
something other
than suspicion?

I've heard
Vyasa
sing your praises
and Mother's
always

saying, *learn
from your brother*;
Narada's face,
which turns
dark every time
he sees me,
glows when he
sets eyes on you.

But what use is
all that to me?
You're only
interested
in scribing
weighty books
and carrying
out errands
for important
people, like
our mother.
What do you
care for
small fry like me?

Why would
my love pangs
move your heart,
which moves
mountains
and oceans and

the whole universe
when it is stirred?

Don't mind me,
I'm only the
foolish younger
brother,
the same one
you beat with
a clever trick
all those years
ago, when he
was at his
most foolish.

Just go on
with the rest
of the universe,
let me sit here
and talk
to your rat – he
has a sympathetic
ear, and who
knows,
maybe he'll
have some ideas.

I've realised
it's no use
owning the most

magnificent
hills and the
deepest caves, or
being patron to
the best poets
and singers – if
I'm to get help
from you, I have
to be the
Mother of the
Universe,
or its Father,
or the Author
of The Most
Important Book
Ever Written.

Just ignore me,
go do all your
important work,
I won't
get in your way.
I'll just lie down
here and see
if sleep will come.

Dear Reader,
what do you think
happened then?

Tell me, do you
see why the poets
and oracles worship
the tongue
of this god, who
kings Pazhani and
all the worlds' words?

Velan tells his friend the poet about how he feels because Valli is not reciprocating his love

Why's everything so silent?
Why aren't our weavers' looms going
iwishiwishiwish? Why's your voice not
reading a new poem? Why's the flapping
of Paravani's wings not following me?
Why's bamboo not nodding to the
wind's repeated drumming?
Why are Chendur's waves not roaring
in my dreams? Where did it all go?

Where's the sky? There's no sky
up there; is the ground here? Hold me,
don't let me fall. Where are the clouds?
Blue, white, gray, black? Did you steal it
all to put in a poem? Am I in your poem?
Is this a sad poem where the hero dies?
But can I die? Am I not a god? Tell me,
friend, this is your poem. Is there a hole
in the poem's scape? Why's

everything rushing in? What happens
to it, afterwards? I don't know, I can't
hear anything.

Where are the little things that run
and play here? Squirrels, hare,
porcupines, deer? Where? I don't see any.
Paravani, what happened to your feathers?
Where's their emerald and blue and
flashing gold? I can't see. And you?
Why's your face so blurred? And my face,
tell me what it looks like, that the river
refuses to look at me now.

But *she* looks at me, the one I wed,
she's always here.
Then, I wanted her face in my eyes
all the time; now, she's here and I
can't look; when the day starts, she calls
my name, she wakes me, she waits, but
I can only think of the other one, Valli,
who stares at me, eyes sharp, like a
one-horned boar that will take off,
but if you don't stop, will turn and strike.

How bright is her skin, my friend,
you should put it in a poem: sun lights
its shades, like on old stones, moss.
When she walks, leaves rustle and shake,

when she talks, the fish in the river leap,
when I catch sight of her eyes, I hear
the scamper of animal feet and
my heart's drum slows its festival beat.

What am I to do, tell me? If we
don't do something, the world will
burn up in my guts, and we can never
get it back, not even if Uncle turns into
that boar again. Tell me what to do,
hold my hand, hold me, hold me,
I'm going to fall. Am I going blind,
blind and deaf? I see nothing, I hear…
but wait, I heard that!
What was that sound? Turn this way,
are you crying? Why are you crying?

Don't cry, my friend,
take my hand, take me away from
her home;
I can't bear to be here and not
have her want me beside her.
Why can't you write a happier poem?
In which she and I are one?
And the world is in its place?

What the peacock said to Ganesha about his brother's lovesickness

My Lord, your brother's
lovesickness is becoming
impossible: ever since he saw
Valli, at the archery contest,
he's being most unreasonable.
He refuses food, then says
he's hungry and wants to go
pick figs on her hill.
He claims hot water's making
him weak and wakes at dawn
to go bathe in the hill stream.
And now he wants grass mats,
no doubt woven with grass
from her hill, because
suddenly
'soft mattresses are bad
for a warrior's body.'

My Lord, your brother's
lovesickness is becoming

impossible. It's days since
he came to the poets' assembly
and you know it's the spring
festival and poets have come
from all over, with a whole
year's worth of poems they
have waited to have him
read and approve.
And all he says is,
'I can't bear poetry now:
tell them to come back next year.'

My Lord, your brother's
lovesickness is becoming
impossible. Three days ago,
he screamed at the rooster
for breaking a dream in
which, following *her* eyes,
he was just about to see
what she was looking at.
What am I to say
to your mother when
she asks why no one's
waking on time: the rooster
you see, flew off in a huff
and hasn't been seen since.

My Lord, your brother's
lovesickness is becoming

impossible. He's forgetting
everything – yesterday,
he came up so close to me,
I could see the emerald and
gold of my feathers in his
eyes, but he just stood there,
his eyes a swirl of colours,
and it took me a moment to
realise he could not recall
my name or what it was he
had wanted me for.

My Lord, your apathy
is becoming unforgiveable.
Are your elephant ears
not privy to all the world's
secrets? Do you not know
what Valli is thinking?
Will she not return our
Kumaran's love?
My Lord, can't you go
and tell her that
your brother, Lord of
Pazhamudircholai – and
of this peacock driven
mad by his antics – is
waiting on her, for a
look, a word?
You'll make a better

messenger than I, for while
I'm a silly bird, you possess
the gravitas of an elephant.

A triptych on love: about the poet, the man she's fallen in love with & the Lord of Pazhani

He

On
the high hill, the
god's two wives
could tell he was
bothered about
something; they asked
him again and again,
but he shook his head
and went away. How
could he tell them that
his poet, and the man
she was in love with,
made him want to be
human?

she

whenever
she was stuck,
He,
the god
with the two
wives, seemed
to know how
to make her love
poem move.
It was,
she thought,
as if
He was human.

he

he was only
human, he knew,
all too human,
but when she,
the poet – who had
told him that she had
tried not to fall in
love with him –
and He, her god,
who lived as
husband to two wives,

on that high hill,
came to visit him,
he often found
himself forgetting
that one of them
was not
human.

MAKING DEALS

Of Singaravelan of Mayilai

Our first sighting of Singaravelan, Lord of Pazhani, the poet's friend

People ask me,
when you first looked
down
from your high hill and
saw me,
what did you see
that brought you
down
to seek me out?

Did you see another
woman,
womanly as any
other –
who c/would make eyes,
speak softly,
step gently, and
be sturdy enough to

bear the weight of
your love's interest?

Or

did you see another
poet:
well-versed as all
others,
who would shut her
eyes, not speak,
run furiously if you
got in the way, and
be sharp enough to
verse your love's
episodes?

We all know the answer,
Singaravelare,
for here you are,
again
muddying in a love-
slush, and I, clear,
on the green bank,
poeming it all down.
Again.
Let's keep it that way,
you be the enchanter,
go make eyes,

go speak silken words,
make tricky promises
you can worm your
way out of,
and I will be the
poet.

Write for you?
You mean, write your
love notes? And poems
in praise? Are you joking?
Don't you know – *the
whole town knows* –
I'm working on a set
of a thousand poems
and have a deadline
to be done before the
year ends. What do you
mean, set that aside?
No, it pays me nothing,
but it is what I want to
do, and it'll be the
masterpiece that gets
me into the great
assembly. Put in a word?
No, I don't want your
recommendation,
I will get in on my own
merit. What! What do

you mean, how am I
sure I will make it? You
better go now, my friend,
you get your peacock to
sing your praises,
or that rooster with a
voice that can't be
stopped.
I'm not your court poet
to be told what to write.
Oh, that's what you
think, is it? No, I don't
want a retainer
from you, let me just be
the *struggling poet*,
and yes,
a woman at that.

Velare,
go now, I think you've
said enough.
But before you go,
hear this:
I'm not going to forget this,
and by my word, I promise,
you – neither will you.

The bet

Ah ha! Velare, it's you!
I was wondering who would
come knocking at my door
this early – even the beggar
sleeps late, in this cold.

So, were you just passing
by and thought you would
look in on me?
Or were you shopping
in the neighbourhood
and decided
to see if I needed anything?

Oh yes, come in, come in,
don't mind me, I'm
just a struggling poet
and a woman at that,
why should I sleep
late?

So, now that you're inside
and seated in comfort,

albeit
on a poor grass mat, not
what you're used to up
there on grand Pazhani hill,
and I've given you
water and fruit,
are you going to tell me
what you came for?
Or do you want me to
wash your feet and offer
worship with leaves
and flowers?
I could, if you like,
but don't expect me to
drink that water,
my glorious Lord,
that's the privilege of the
men.

What? Speak up! I can't
hear what
you're saying.
You lost a bet? What bet?
An antadi bet? Why
should you lose
any bet that has to do
with words?
Aren't you the best poet
in all the worlds?

What? The bet is with
your father?
And he has said that
whoever gets the new
word
I'm going to make up
today and uses it to
start the set, will win?

Well, I haven't made up
anything; perhaps,
if you'd let me sleep,
my mind would function.
No, my Lord, I don't want
your ring or your
waistband
or your armlet – I don't want
anything that you have,
or wait, did you say I could
have
whatever I ask for?
Then, how about a ride
across the sky on your
emerald
peacock, out there
over green fields that the
sun will shortly rise in?
No? Yes?
No?

Let me go back to sleep.
Yes?
Well then, I will just have to
make up that word now,
won't I?
Singaravelare, my friend,
the things
I do for you.

She explains to her mother why Singaravelan has turned up at the crack of dawn, outside her door

This is
Singaravelan,
the great Lord of Pazhani;
he also claims to be my friend
and sometimes I think he is;
he's come looking for me because
he's in a mess of some sort.
Mother, I'm going to leave you here
and go with him; will you please
finish this meal I'm cooking
for you, Father, little brother and sister?
No, Mother,
I cannot stay, for when he
comes to me, it's because he's tried
everything else.
And though I may make light of it
when I talk, the friendship of this one

I will not risk losing, ever. Let me go now,
Mother, and in case I do not return
by the time of your departure,
let me embrace you all now.
Father,
won't you come again
when you go to Madurai to get stocks
for the season? Sometimes I miss you all,
when the rains start and I'm stuck
in this house, I remember how I would
fold and pin jackfruit leaves into
boats for the little ones.
How the seasons have passed.
No, Mother,
you know I cannot return;
I'm not a leaf to be folded, pinned and
floated. My life is here, with
the Lord of Pazhani hill,
with his follies, his taciturnity,
his moodiness and his undying
friendship – which, though I make light of it,
I know means the world to him;
should I need him, he would drop
everything and be
here in a trice. Yes, yes, my friend, coming!
How impatient you get! I know you're the
great Lord of Pazhani and I'm only a
struggling poet and a woman at that, but
I'm a daughter taking leave of her parents,

an older sister embracing her little siblings, give me a moment to do that. But what do you know of such things? You stalked away from all bonds so long ago. No, no, nothing, I'm coming now, for all bonds pale before this bond of friendship with you. Why am I whispering, you ask, Mother? Because I can't afford to let him hear that last thing I said – he will use it to his advantage. Let him think I take this friendship as lightly as he takes the rules of the world's etiquette.

Bailing him out

What happened, my dear
Singaravelare,
what have you
gone and done now?
Every time you come down from
your high hill,
you're sure to get into
some muddle, and then
you come straight to me.
Don't you have friends
who are worldly wise and
have the means to help you?
What can I,
a struggling poet
and a woman at that,
do
that the mighty Lord of Pazhani
hill can't?

So speak up, Velare
what have you done now?

I know what this is about,
it's about the
waistband you sneaked out of
your wife's jewel box to give
that hunter's maid
you're so besotted with,
isn't it?

If you had told me then,
I would have told you that
your mother-in-law had a
spell put on it
from the moment the
wedding was fixed,
for, you see, she too
had heard of your exploits.

Your peacock came yesterday
to tell me what's been happening.
Is it really true, my great Lord,
that every time someone
passes the hunter girl,
your wife's waistband calls
out, saying *Someone help me,*
I belong to the wife
of the Lord of Pazhani hill;
he stole me away from her
and now only he can get
me out of this?

I'm sorry I can't keep a
straight face, this is the funniest
thing I've heard: it's
one of your best, Velare.
I want to tell it to everyone.

What do you want me to do,
anyway? What? Undo the spell?
What makes you think a poor
poet has the power to do all that?
Your mother told you?
Well then, I can't say no, can I?
Take me to your beloved, then,
that green kurati, she of the bright
eyes and strong arms,
the one that's turned you into
a thief,
and let me speak to the spell.

Singaravela,
my friend, the things I do for you!

Dressing up

Oh my! Velare!
What's this?
You're here again? That's
twice this week, isn't it?
The last time you were here,
you came
before the sun rose
and today, the sly moon
has already risen. I
know you don't think of
these things, but if the
neighbours
see you, they're sure to
gossip, so come on inside,
tell me what the matter is
and be gone quickly.

Would you like a drink of
water, my Lord, or some of
this kanji? The kanji? Yes,
it's my dinner
but that's okay,
we can share

it if you like, you know I'm
only a poet – I don't really
work,
and anyway, today,
while measuring out the rice,
my hand slipped and I
ended up adding an extra fistful.

Now that you're not hungry
anymore, will you tell me
what's wrong?
Of course something's
wrong. Don't I know that
look of yours
well enough by now?
Quickly now, let's get this
over with, you really can't
stay here long – I may be
only a struggling poet
but I'm a woman
and women, they say, must
protect their reputations.

What is it? Come on, it can't
be worse than the time
they captured
your peacock to prove you
were there, in the women's
quarters, or that business of

your promising to let that
girl – what was her name?
try your vel in exchange for a
kiss.
Is it worse? With you,
one never can tell, you have
such a need for drama.
Out with it!
I can't stand the suspense.
What! No! Really! Well,
well, you've got to keep your
promise or you'll lose face.

What's my role here, though?
He's your uncle and
everybody knows he indulges
your every whim.
So just go ask him – tell him
he only has to appear and
disappear, he doesn't need
to wait for introductions!
Oh! He said that? I suppose it
is true – your mother can be
unreasonable when she's
angered – and I can see she
would definitely not want
her brother to appear
cross-dressed

before some strange girl,
especially if the girl happens
to be her son's girlfriend.

So then, there's nothing to be
done, is there? Me?
What can I do, my great Lord
of Pazhani hill, remember, I'm
the struggling poet, and, oh
dear, just a woman. No,
no, I can't be bribed with
peacock rides or your many
ornaments.
A kiss! You've got to be out of
your mind. Not me, Velare,
no kisses. I certainly
don't want any of that.
But maybe, if you promise to
take a break from your romps
long enough to come
and write with me as you've
been promising, I might
reconsider.
You will?
But I want it in writing,
with your signature in bold.

Now that we're settled on the

terms of this barter, come call
your peacock and let's be off;
let's go find your uncle,
he owes me
for a favour I did him – no, I
can't say what, I've learnt the
hard way never to trust you
with secrets, who knows what
you'll trade it for – no, Velare,
I really won't tell you what it
was I helped that uncle of
yours with, no, don't look at
me like that – I'm not one of your
women. Oh, okay, for friendship's
sake, I'll tell you this much: it,
too, had to do with women and
with words. Now, come, let's go
and sort this out. The things
I do for you, my
friend, Singaravelan of Mayilai.

VIP

This one, brother, this parchment's the one I
will take, but I have to tell you – your work's a
bit shoddy; your father did this with such care,
such attention – the curing, the liming, all of it;
he himself went each time to pick the limestone,
then he sat for days, coughing in lime dust, to
make sure it was powdered as fine as it should
be. He made the brine and always used rubbing
salt that was a season old. And then, after the
scraping – which he let only the practiced workers
do – he had this thing of soaking the skins again,
in thin brine, before washing and drying. And the
stretching! The care he took with the stretching!
And look at this! This hasn't been stretched
enough, it's not as crisp as it ought to be! You
don't check before cutting the parchments from
their frames? Clearly your heart's not in this.
Maybe it's better if I just do my own curing, from
start – I can't use this without some more scraping
and then I will have to do a couple of rounds of
wiping over with brine and sun-drying. Does your
father mean to come back at all? What? Why're
you gesturing like that? Why this sudden respect?

Stop doing that, put your hands down, I don't want you saluting me – I'm only a poor poet. What? What are you rolling your eyes for? Turn? Turn back? Oh, oh! Velare! You startled me! What are you doing in the marketplace? You really shouldn't be here in this throng and the sting of brine. Come, my friend, let's go somewhere else, I don't want you fainting on me. Brother, why are you looking so bug-eyed, I know this is the Lord of Pazhani, our king and god and all that, but he's my friend, are you not, my dear Singaravelare? Is it too hot here, your face is turning red?

Now that we're out of earshot, what are you doing, following me? I told you, didn't I, that I don't want to see you? When you were doing the rounds of the town yesterday – or should I say, when you were being paraded – in all your silk & velvet finery, your strings of pearls, emeralds & marble-sized diamonds and that turban gleaming like sun, moon, stars and a fire added – you pretended not to notice me, though at our last meeting when I saved you, again, you promised me a ride in your golden chariot, drawn by four-headed Brahma on those horses from heaven. Now go away – if you were ashamed of me yesterday, you must still be, for nothing much has changed since then. What? Brahma refused to stop? You expect me to just believe that? As if he would say no to you! He can't have forgotten how you roughed him up all those years ago. A difficult turn in the road and he could not slow? Oh, come on! What next! Stop your excuses and go away, my great Lord of Pazhani hill, you're too grand for riff-raff like me, not only am I a mere poet, but I'm also a woman. How much worse can it get? You go away now, go to your palace, to your great parents, your invincible brother, your good-looking companion, the peacock, and oh, don't let's forget, the hordes of women all over this busy world – swooning over you. Go to one of them. I've no time for you – I've a poem to finish and a parchment to re-cure because that young man, unlike his father, doesn't do his job properly – just like another young man I could name.

What? Don't touch me, I've told you before, don't touch me – I don't like it, and what will people say, let go of my hand now, Velare. What's this? What are you giving me? Oh! A roll of parchment! And so perfectly cured, so thin and crisp! This is, oh, what's this! Another roll inside the first, and, oh, one more, and I don't believe this, there's another roll here. What's this, my friend? Magic? What? Made by Chitragupta, you say? Oh my! And these rolls will never end? Oh, but what about that old man and his parchments? He enjoys his work, and he and I have a good relationship;

I can't stop buying from him. What? When? How did you know? Oh yes, I forget you are a god and you would know if someone dies. Oh, but these are so lovely, soft, yet crisp, and so thin they won't crinkle in the rolling. Thank you, my friend, but I am not over my anger yet and I don't want to see you for some time. Eh? What's this, now? Another gift? You're clearly trying to bribe me; of course, you think poets are soft targets for your charm – not me, not me. Here, take this back; just look at it? Okay, let me see. My god – no, not you, don't smirk – these styluses are beautiful! What are they made of? Silver and brass melded? Isn't that what I told you last week I would get, if I ever came into money? You remembered? But who made these? It's such an incredibly difficult process, my friend, the stylus-maker at Madurai, once explained it to me. Who made these? Who? Vishwakarma? Ha ha ha, why would I even ask! Well, at least some good has come of knowing an important person! Thank you. Yes, I am keeping these and you're forgiven. Again, my friend, again. The things I do for you, dear Singaravelan of Mayilai. And now tell me, why're you here; what am I saving you from today?

I have to protect my reputation

I don't understand you, Velare,
how could you do this? Haven't I
told you not to do things that draw
the neighbours' attention? And here
you are, on my rooftop, planting
your rooster banner atop the
chimney and circling overhead
on your noisy peacock.
All because I asked you to wait
while I finished the line I was working
on? Look, now you've drawn
a right royal crowd of them,
standing and gawking. As it is,
they think I'm strange, and now this.
They will ask why it is that a god,
known for his knotty escapades
with women, should be circling over
my house if it's all on the level.
What, they will ask, with that look,
have you been doing? And to think
the only scandalous thing I do is –
I write.

Anyway, now that you've come
down, let's deal with your problem.
No, no, not in the house, not on
your life, that's all they need now.
Let's just go sit under
that tree, that big one with the
bark that cools
the brain – mine certainly
needs cooling. No, Velare,
don't smile, I know all this
comes from
your thinking I'm jobless.
No, no, don't do that, it makes
you look more idiotic.
I'm not one of
your women to swoon over that.
Now quick, tell me what the
problem is: I want you out of
my sight as soon as possible.

Yes, I remember the feast
Indra threw last week to
celebrate his release from that
awful but deserved curse.
Yes, I heard accounts of it. What
about it, though? What
could you possibly have done
there? Weren't your parents there?
Ha ha ha! Really? You did that?
How Indra deserved that! He got

what was coming to him.
But wait, how did you change
into a woman? You couldn't have
done it on your own, you told me
your mother put that little bind on
your shape-changing
after you were found in the ladies'
quarters, in a woman's body.
Urvashi helped you? Well, well,
the plot thickens,
but I thought she was Indra's
favoured one? Rambha?
Oh, yes, that enmity is legendary.
But wait,
so Urvashi helped you transform
into a woman, but how could she
override your mother's binding?
Not transform, then?
Oh, I see, you traded bodies?
So your body and hers, then
your spirit, mind, what do you call
these things for gods?
Don't smile, don't smile.
So your body had her mind and hers
had yours? Then?
You went to the heavenly gardens
– wait, don't tell me, I don't
want to know. So you did whatever
it was you did there, seems simple
enough, so, what happened?

Urvashi caused trouble? For once,
it was someone else. What? In your
body? She accosted Indra and did
what? Oh my god! Sorry, sorry,
Velare, I can't help laughing.
Don't you find it funny?
Imagine Indra's shock when 'you'
when you – poor man. I wonder if he
was flattered that the handsomest,
most desirable man in all creation
was making a pass at him?
How did he realise it was Urvashi?
She told him? Let me guess
what's coming – he cursed
you? I can tell from your face it was
a serious curse,
but if it was only your body & Urvashi's
spirit, wouldn't the curse be hers?
By name, is it, so he said,
I hereby curse Singaravelan, son of
Siva and Parvathy – no, no, don't
throw that, I'll stop laughing. Tell me
about the curse. Oh, no wonder you
look so upset. So, every time you're with
a woman and things are hotting up,
you'll turn into Urvashi?
Velare, you should consider keeping
the curse, you need a curse like this.
It'll make you see what being a
woman means; maybe it'll make you

write, if you have time away from
your distractions.

Anyway, he's Indra, king of the gods,
and he's cursed you. What can I
possibly do? I'm just a struggling poet
and *a… a… my god, I can't stop laughing*
and a woman at that, see, so
useless. What can I do to make
him take back the curse? Why are you
looking at me like that? I hope
you're not going to suggest that I…
What? Write a poem to him in
the metre I made up last week?
No, that metre is not meant
for… Velare! What
are you doing? Stop that!
You're a god, you mustn't do
such things, please stop, please
get up, yes yes yes, I will.
I'll write about that self-absorbed,
vain creature. Thank god
I already wrote a poem to your
brother in this new metre, yesterday.
You really live life on the edge, my
friend, and maybe that's why I… okay,
let me go start on that poem.
The things I do for you, Singaravelan,
Lord of beauteous Pazhani & of poetry.

An impressive body of writing

Velare, you haven't heard a word I said!
– and now I sound like a wife – you've
such a knack for getting in the way of my
work and then they'll keep me out of the
assembly, saying, not enough work to
sit with these hard-working poets, who
have such an impressive body of writing.
Sometimes, I wonder if it's because I'm
a woman – do they still think you and I are,
are… don't smile, don't smile, you just
wasted half my day with your chatter.
I'm so irritated with you, go away; why do
you have to come and sit in my house,
remember I'm just a *struggling poet and
a woman at that.*

You have palaces all over the world, the
heavens vie to host you, and then there
are the bed chambers of all those women
who say they'd do anything to have you
in their beds. Go away, go home, go trouble
your mother, go inspire those men, go
into the marketplace and stop trade,

go to the kalari and stop their practice,
stand there and bask in the admiration in
their eyes, all turned to your beaut – you're
gloating, don't smile like that, I accidentally
started to say *beautiful*, your face isn't
beautiful, it's just plain boring, look at it,
so smooth, not even the hint of a scratch –
have you not aroused any woman so
much, her fingers running down your
cheeks, fondling your ear, stopped and
held, leaving you eternally marked? Ha!
That's it! All this talk of valour and this
aura of the dandy is to cover up the fact
that you can't do it. I knew it, that's why
you keep going off to battles and hunting
expeditions, that's why you get up from
your seat in Kataragama and Nallur and
go off to Siyambalawa – they say you're
gathering yourself, but now I know, you're
crying over your lack of manliness. That's
why you're not marrying, that's why you've
let me... Oh no! you did it again, didn't
you? You made me write a poem that
none of those men would ever write, and
now, what are you doing? Hey! Get your
hands off me, no touching, Vela, that's our
deal, remember? What? Your chain? Why?
Didn't your uncle give you this? No, no, no
I don't want it, take it back, in any case,

everybody knows it's yours, I won't be able
to wear it. Here, my friend, take it, wait, I'll
put it back round your neck, but you can get
me back my seat in the assembly, just tell
Nakkeerar it was you who put that line
into my poem last week, get him to dismiss
the *disciplinary action* against me, tell him
to dismiss my suspension. You'll do that?
I have these six new poems I want to read,
and this time, Singaravela, of great Mayilai,
my friend, I'll read my own work, you stay
far away from me, and my poems.

Making deals

i
Vela,
if you want me
to pretend
to your mother that
you were with me
last night,
engrossed
in editing my poems,
you'll have to fly me
to Madurai, where
he will also come
to hear the festival
concerts – the one who
my traitor heart has left
me for – and you'll write
the poem that Nakkeerar
expects me to read
in the assembly
on Friday.

ii

Vela,
if you want me
to go to
Valli in the forest,

you'll
have to
take me to

Tirumal in the milk.

You want me
to ask her
how you
may win her;
I want to ask him
how they won him,
all those women:
the poets.

God knows I need
that information
to win *him* –
the one I'm in
love with, the one
who's appearing
in my poems.

iii

Vela,
if you want me
to go ask Valli's
friends what she
said about your
gift,

you'll
have to tell me
what it meant
when *he* – the
one who
stole my heart –
said, in my hearing,
'I have no one
to carry messages.'

iv

Vela,
you tell me
I'm a poet, and
I should be able to
look into time
and
tell you if Valli
will say
Yes.

I'm saying
you're
a god, you should
be able to tell me
what I
would have
seen, had I held
his gaze,
when I saw
him looking – the one
who has my heart.

v

Vela,
if you want me
to hide behind trees
and tell you
if Valli looks
your way as she
passes by,
you'll
have to
part time's curtain
and tell me if
he continued
to look – the one
from the previous
two poems – till he
couldn't see me
anymore.

vi

Vela,
if you want me
to write you
a poem that
stirs Valli's
heart
and makes her
dream of you,
you'll
have to
make *him*
– the one who my
heart followed home –
dream of
my poem and
write to me.

vii

Vela,
if you want me
to help you steal
Valli's parrot, then be
the hero who *finds* it –
you'll
have to
make him – the one
I've fallen in love with –
parrot

your actions:
make him want to
steal my heart.

viii

Vela,
if you want me
to go tell
your brother you're
dying of love for
Valli,
you'll
have to
go and ask that one,
the one I love:

Brother, isn't it
time you
were dying of
love
for my friend,
the poet?

ix

Vela,
if you want me
to tell Deva you're
going to the hills
to help me find

indigo for my inks,
you'll have to
melt
the rocky hill
of *his* heart,
the one I have
fallen in love
with, and
fill it with
the indigo of
my ink.

x

Vela,
if you want me
to tell
Valli about
Deva, and Deva
about Valli,
you'll
have to promise
me, you won't
ever tell *him*,
the one who
thieved my
heart away,
what I said that day
we saw him,
come to make
festival purchases,

his woman on
his right.

xi
Vela,
if you want me
not to snigger
when you're pretending
to be helpless
with the
bow and arrow,
in Valli's forest,
hoping she'll offer
to show you how,
then
you'll have to stop
sniggering when
I'm trying to find
a seat where *he* can
see me (the one
who I've given
my heart to),
my hands bangled
my eyes blackened
and the neckline
of my blouse, not
'plunging dangerously
to the waist',
as you put it, but
just till here, see.

Oof! Sometimes I
forget you're a man.
VelA! No! You
can't *see*.

xii

Vela,
you want me
to seduce her
brother
so that he
will persuade
Valli
to consider you
kindly?

If that's what
you want me
to do,
you go
persuade
him
 – that one,
who has
stolen my heart –
to stop treating
me
like a sister:
make him

want
to seduce me.

xiii
Vela,
if
you want me
to go to
Valli
and tell her such
stories about
you
that she will want
to come running to
you, then
you'll have to
promise me
you'll go to
his
town – yes,
that one that
I've fallen in
love with –
befriend
him and tell
him things about
me that will
make him wish
I would run after him.

xiv

Vela,
if you want me
to fill in for you
in the assembly,
in your body,
while you go off
with mine, you've
got to swear, by the
one you're pursuing,
that you will go
nowhere near
him – the one who
I wish would pursue
me – because
you never know
when he might
realise there's
more to me than
my fond heart.

xv

Vela,
if you want me
to write you more
notes, we've got to
sort out something
first: I resent you
accusing me of

making eyes at
him – yes, yes, that
one who has
my heart.
How is it
one rule for you
and another for me?
The way your eyes
behave when Valli
is near, anyone
would think you're
having a fit.
My eyes don't spin or
dance,
they're hospitable –
they'd put out a mat
for anyone, even you.
What can I do, if *he*
thinks it's a bed?

xvi

Vela,
if you want me
to put this poem
on hold, to help
you with a costume
for the party
Valli's father is
throwing for

warriors,
then you'll have to
go and costume
his heart – the one I
can't stop putting into
my poems – in warrior
garb, make it want
to come and tourney
for my affection.

xvii

Vela,
if you want me
to give up
chasing him, the one
who stole my heart,
let's make one thing
clear: you will also
have to give up the chase
 – no going after Valli,
with stories of her being
the *soul*, and you,
whatever it is that souls
unite with. At least
my heart is real,
you can hear it and feel it.
And even *see* it – when
he is near – leaping
inside my blouse.

xviii
Vela,
if you want me
to put your name
in all the poems
I'm writing, then you
will have to make
him register –
yes, Vela, the one
I long for – how
his name would ring
and resound,
like one
of your incomparable
names,
with perfect stress,
if it joins with mine.

xix
Vela,
if you want me
to forget about
him – the one I love,
till the poetry festival
is over, because you
can't bear to lose
face if 'your' poet
doesn't win,
then you must agree

to make him feel,
in my absence, as
if he's a poem
waiting to be paged.

xx

Vela,
if you want me
to put aside
my 'gaudy' sarees,
and don your saffron
– and I know you must
have made a bet over
this – then you've got
to promise me that
you'll put a rainbow in
his eyes – the one I'm
hopelessly in love with.
I want to ensure that
when he looks at me,
he'll not see *saffron,*
think I've become
'one of the Lord's
people'
and go away.
You think you're so
smart, Vela – don't
forget, I know your ways.

xxi

Vela,
if you want me
to prove that I love
you more than I
love him – the one
who's also in these
poems – then you'll
have to prove that
you love me more
than all those men
in the assembly,
who have been
crowned with titles
of 'Leader' while
I'm merely called
'Kandhan's poet'.

xxii

Vela,
you want me
to pretend to be
your latest? Are you
stupid or what?
But of course,
you are:
maravadivela.

Every
body knows
we're best friends.
Who's going to
believe we've
suddenly
become lovers?
And anyway,
I'm sure they've all
seen the way my face
burns and my chest
almost bursts out
of my blouse when
he is nearby, the one
I couldn't help
falling in love with.

Okay, okay
have it your way,
I'll pretend
to be your lover –
ugh, stop that, Vela,
no need to hold me
so tight.
But you'll have to
ensure *he* is
out of town
when we're doing
all this pretending;
if he sees us,

and thinks it true,
his eyes – which're
just beginning to
send me sidelong
glances (that take off
even before they land)
will never turn to
me again.

Yes, Vela,
my face is
burning and
my chest bursting,
just like yours. Don't
you see? We're truly
in the same boat.
We two could fit
that description:
made for each other.

xxiii

Ayya!
You want me
to call you Ayya now?
Vela, you're my friend,
you've been my
companion since
I can remember.
How can I call you
Ayya?

You do know that
Ayya means
   Master,
   Lord &
   Father,
don't you?
Yes, yes, I know your
devotees call you
like that, but I can't
call you
Father, *Lord* or Master,
because you're my friend.

Okay, okay, have it your way,
there's no point in
reasoning with you
when you're like this.

But here's the deal: if you
want me to play this role
convincingly, in front of
your visiting in-laws, you've
got to get off your high
hill, er, horse, I mean,
and come with me
to Madurai and get me
into the great assembly
full of old men, who
call each other

Ayya, Ayya,
and who look at me
and turn away,
because I am not a man
and they don't know
what to call me.
You'll have to show
them how to address
one who's
no Ayya, but who
writes just as well
as any one of those.

xxiv
Vela,
if you want me
to
believe you're
really pleased
with my poem,
and are not
saying that just
to get me to write
your messages
to Valli,
you have to go
to him – *the one I'm
dying of love for –*
and read to him from

the notes I've
written for you, so that
he feels there's
nothing he wants more
than to get messages
from me.
You'll also
have to promise
that you'll be,
when the time comes,
the ideal messenger.
Yes, Vela, that means
you'll have to write
notes for me.
I drive a hard bargain?
My dear Vel*ayya*,
anyone who knows you
like I do, will
know that's the
only way
to deal with you.

Sealing the deal

Vadivela,

you're telling me you're willing to put it all down in writing? Really?
Give me one reason to believe it's as it appears to be. Better think before
you answer – I'm in no mood for banter, after what you've done. You've what?
Turned over a new leaf? And what leaf would that be, pray? You gave your
word: *no tricks*?
Since when? Your birthday? That was six months ago. Ha! Not a chance!
Wasn't the business of our Madurai poet 'losing' his manuscript just
three months ago? And hold on, my suspension from the assembly – no,
Vela, don't turn your face away – six months haven't passed since then,
let me count: Deepavali, and then the festival of your brother, our temple
theru… yes! It was only five months ago. What do you mean, *you* did
nothing? Let's call your friend, the vain peacock, let him be the judge of

whether you did *nothing*. Ayya, Paravani, Ayya, could you come here for a few minutes?

Vela,

let me tell your friend here, what you did – exactly as it was – and you stay quiet, Vela. So, Paravani, do you recall my suspension from the assembly *five* months ago? Yes, it was during the annual poetry week. The assembly had finally Yes-ed my induction & I was there, like all of the 'new' poets, to participate in the trial-by-votes that determines our seating order in the assembly. You know how it works, no? All poets-elect bring poems, on a topic given prior, and all our entries are dropped into that box, and they call for readers from the audience, who pick a poem at random, and read. And the panel judges your poem, from the reading. Right? You know that. But you know what this *friend* of mine, the great Lord of Pazhani, did? You weren't there, but if you had been, you'd have been as shocked as I was. He, this one here, telling me he turned over a new leaf *six* months ago, he came to my house the evening before the event, he took my poem saying, he would do *one last check of the poem's time measures*.

And I, trusting fool that I am, didn't think to check my own manuscript,
when he gave it back the next morning: if I had, I would have known that your
Lord Guha, the great patron, had inserted such clever, shocking similes
about the way *men* write poetry, into my poem, and got the whole thing
copied out in writing exactly like mine. You can imagine my state, can't you,
when the reader got to that part? It set off such an uproar in the audience,
which rose like waves in a full-moon tide, roaring with glee.

Paravani, you have no idea how they chastised me, that day, in their stiff
man-language: it set my teeth on edge; then, they huddled and whispered,
while the crowds called out for more, and announced my suspension from
the assembly. Even now, when I think of it, I start to sweat – how I left the
hall, so meekly, my chest a cauldron of boiling protest and my eyes stinging,
I knew if I said anything during the probation period,
they would use that to rescind my membership. What do you mean, Vela,
why do I want to be a member? You know all the poets worth a word are in
there, as are all the best critics and patrons, from all over. Paravani, wait,

don't go, you're supposed to be the judge here. Pah! He's run off; so scared of you, Vela, at least now, admit you're a tyrant.

What? Yes, I know your mother came to the assembly then, after someone ran to her, and she sorted out that mess and yes, I know that it's a delicate matter because the men in the assembly are all your father's chelas. I also know you staged this performance so that your mother could come there, and tell them all off. She could insist that they undertake some long due introspection, amend the bylaws so it would be mandatory to increase the number of women in the assembly, and for half of the judges to be women. I know those are the things you wanted, but why me? Why me? Why do you have to use me to make your point? Every time? *Reliable*? *Dependable*? Bah! You're supposed to be the reliable one, you're the god, remember, and I'm the poet, human and frail. I'm supposed to depend on you, to rely on you and bask in your appreciation, but you? You must put me through tests, challenges, dares. Ah! The sound? Yes, that sound is the sound of my blood boiling, my Lord. Why must I constantly anticipate your designs on me?

I believe that this move is proof that our relationship has grown, proof that
it has matured, proof that we two have matured.

Let's write this contract, by all means. Now that I am a master poet – as if
I wasn't before the assembly certified me – I think we should make our
arrangement more professional: you let me set the terms that will stop
you breathing down my neck each time I'm to write something for you;
it'll stop you sending your spies to check on me, it will stop you raising an
alarm if I so much as take a breath, let alone pause, to rest my thoughts.
My Lord, let's sign this deal.
But, wait a moment, wait! Why are you smiling? I won't proceed till we
deal with that smile; your *karma-negating, benevolent, life-saving
loving* smile, for which I can think of many, more appropriate synonyms.

Your devotees, your parents & your two wives; singers, oracles, lovers,
kadamba trees, clouds, the oceans, why, all creation, may long for this
smile of yours, my friend, but not I: I have spent a life, and several
manuscripts, at the receiving end of that smile. I dread to even think of

what clauses you've thought up for this wonderful contract. It is a trap
I certainly don't want to let myself tripfall into now. So, my dear friend,
Singaravela, Lord of Pazhani, of all – of alphabets, the rules of grammar,
of time measures, and let's not forget: of rude tricks, sly riddles, jokes
and sundry other whatnots, let's just let it be for now.
What is it the wise ones have said:
Better the tricks one knows than those one'll never learn?

Afterword

The women in these poems were carefully written – indeed, the little rework I did on the manuscript was to underline their willfulness and strength; some of the women are poets, some are scribes, editors and messengers, others are warriors and scholars, some run households while others run kingdoms, and they are all acquainted, in varying degrees of involvement, with the god, Murugan. Some of these women are hopelessly in love with him and he is hopelessly in love with some of them; between them, there is a mutual give-and-take of flirtation, seduction, wooing, uniting, parting, pining, beseechment, surrender and always, a straining to get on with writing.

Roughly one-third of *Offer Him All Things, Charred, Burned & Cindered*, is either sutras – listing Murugan's attributes – or guide poems – advice from older poets to novices selected into the god's retinue of scholars, singers and poets. Both these are, for the most part, in un-gendered voices. Then there are messenger poems, many of which are sent by women in love with the god, desolated by his absence, begging him to come back; in these episodes, the women are unable to write or do anything other than long for him and dictate poems and messages to him. They often talk of giving Murugan everything that is theirs, surrendering their attention entirely to him; this surrender is qualified – it is a passing mood for that time in the relationship and it is a gesture made to one who has repeatedly made this exact same gesture to them.

There is a paralleling of what the women do and what the god does. One woman, wrung out with longing for Murugan, tells her friend, 'Promise him my life: all my manuscripts, my inks, pens, my lexicons.' The god, tormented by unrequited love, says he will die of this longing, and asks his friend, 'Why can't you write a happier poem? In which she and I are one? And the world is in its place?'

The women and the men are written with equal parts willfulness and surrender, love and longing, skill and intuition and, of course, playfulness in speech and action. The toughest and possibly most exciting part of writing these poems was figuring out how to make the god pliant to the will of the women, their intellect, their love, their writing, without weighting too lightly on the side of his charm, the enchantment of his attentiveness, his inherent allure.

I was watching an old film's song sequence in which the revered Tamizh poet, Auvaiyyar, played by K.B. Sunderambal, sings to Murugan – he is youthful and handsome, his smile is radiant, and his sparkling wit and charm are making the old woman smile; she is sturdy, white-haired, saffron-clad, full of authority and quick speech – when I realized what a convenient figure she is. Auvaiyyar has un-gendered herself, instantly transformed through a boon into an old woman, who is made even more unproblematic and comforting with the title of paatti (grandmother). What if she had been a young woman? What if there had been many young women poets in this god's workshop/assembly? Is it not impossible that all his poets were men and old women?

This song wasn't the only one that affected these poems. There are many others, from some of the lively 'little' traditions of Tamizh – devotional songs, film songs and 'non-weighty' songs in the Carnatic music corpus, that I've heard repeatedly on radio and in concerts, which speak of Murugan playfully, affectionately and familiarly. The Singaravelan of my poems must have been influenced by this song, which indulgently describes how everything he does, he does with an eye to getting what he wants: '*Kaariyakkaaranadi andha Ganapathiyin thambi, Kandhan enum nambi*'. Then, there was that goosefleshingly-lovely *kavadi chindu*, which says that he will sip no nectar, even if it be ambrosia, except that of Valli's lips: '*Valli sevvidhazh aladiniya tellamudumayilan*'. The same song describes how Murugan makes sure that Devayani/Teivanai doesn't get bored with him: '*kunjara anangu avalvidapadi konjimaruvum sarasa ranjita viseda*'.

Countless songs sung by the honey-voiced T.M. Soundararajan, a master of the devotional – who I listen to every morning – which spoke of Murugan's love sagas, his attempts to win the interest and love of the two women who became his wives, and of his dandiness, his flirtations, his dalliances, his shape-shifting, made me eager to put similar gestures and moods into what I was writing, and sometimes led me out of dead-end lines.

An old idea – of adapting/re-imagining archaic Tamizh formats, such as the antadi and atrupadai in English – came back while tracking down rare Tamizh songs I have been hearing contemporary musician Sanjay Subrahmanyan sing. His rendering of the padam, 'netrandhi nerattile', in which the nayika is asking Murugan, 'Yesterday, at dusk, near the stream's bank, who was that woman who came up close and made inviting eyes at you?' made me try padam-like poems, a couple of which are included here.

To these three musicians and to my perspicacious editor Karthika V. K., who waits till I have written the best versions of my poems, I must express my gratitude. As also to Chaitanya, who drove me to Kataragama and who, along with P, accompanied me on repeated visits to the temple there. And to every song I have heard (and to the people who transliterate and translate them into English) about the mercurial god called Skanda in Kataragama and Murugan in Pazhani, who is the life-breath in alphabets, grammars and the work of countless poets, like me.